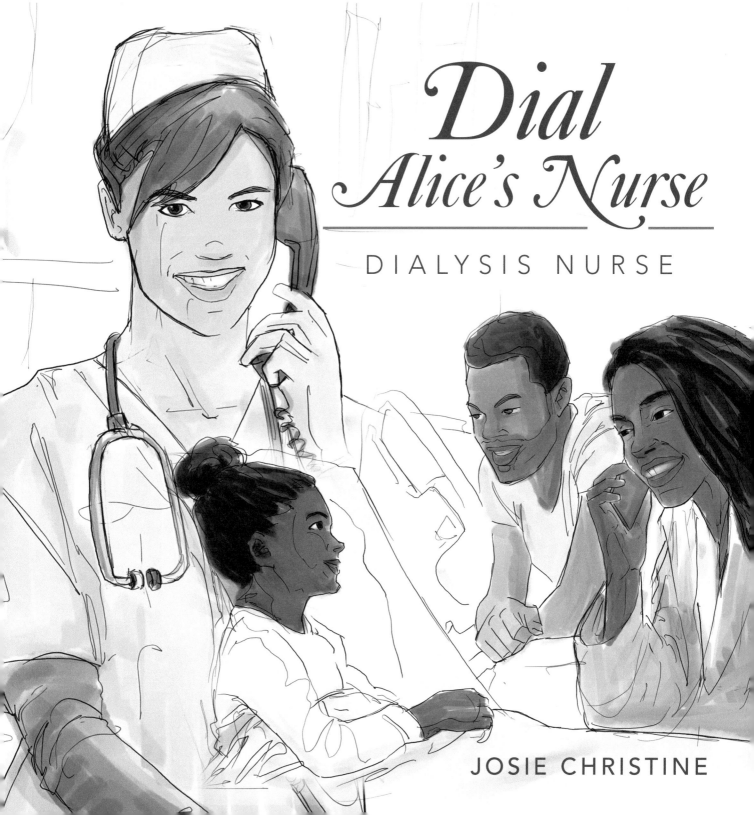

AuthorHouse™
1663 Liberty Drive
Bloomington, IN 47403
www.authorhouse.com
Phone: 1 (833) 262-8899

Because of the dynamic nature of the Internet, any web addresses or links contained in this book may have changed since publication and may no longer be valid. The views expressed in this work are solely those of the author and do not necessarily reflect the views of the publisher, and the publisher hereby disclaims any responsibility for them.

The views expressed in this work are solely those of the author and do not necessarily reflect the views of the publisher, and the publisher hereby disclaims any responsibility for them.

Any people depicted in stock imagery provided by Getty Images are models, and such images are being used for illustrative purposes only. Certain stock imagery © Getty Images.

This book is printed on acid-free paper.

ISBN: 978-1-7283-7274-7 (sc)
ISBN: 978-1-7283-7275-4 (e)

Print information available on the last page.

Published by AuthorHouse 08/31/2020

authorHOUSE®

Dedication Page

I dedicate this story to my nurses, doctors, family, and friends who stood beside me fighting Kidney Disease, Love Jo

Contents

I. *Introduction*

Once upon a time, a young girl named Alice could not believe
She was living with something called "Kidney Disease".
"Kidney failure" is now a part of her life,
Gazing at her parents, this is not right.

Alice was potty trained by age two,
By age five, she forgot how to.
Mom and dad weep as Alice sobs in pain
While the Dialysis Nurse connects her to a machine

II. *Alice Tells Her Story*

"Dialysis, what is that "? Alice said.
My friends will not know what that is.
I hope they still like me, I am a cool kid,
My kidney's failure is not something I did.

I ate my veggies and my fruit,
I obeyed my mom and dad too.
I didn't tell stories or act mean to my friends,
I prayed and prayed at the night end.

I brushed my teeth and I flossed
But that did not fix my kidney loss.
Needles and tubes are now my life-line,
After sitting many hours, I almost feel fine.

WARRIOR

This is my new daily routine,
I feel good now that my blood is clean.
I hope kidney loss does not last long,
I am still kid, although I appear strong.

III. *Alice's Dream*

Every day I daydream about what I might be,
If someone is a donor match for me.
I know I love nurses maybe I'll be one,
My dialysis nurse is smart and fun.

Maybe a teacher or the leader of a nation,
So, I can teach others about organ donation.
Saving a life is the greatest gift,
Learning the facts can erase myths.

One day I will travel without machines,
medicine, doctors, blood, and tubings.
For now, I am a warrior with a big heart.
Waiting on the call, "we have your spare part"!

IV. *Alice the Warrior*

Kids Wellness Camp Friends came to play.
Brock the broccoli, Apple Jackie, Banana Baby, and Little Grapes.
My Food Friends show me fruits and veggies I can eat.
So, I do not get sick or itchy when I jump to my feet.

My Dialysis nurse said Kidney Disease affects all of us.
You are a warrior Alice I look up to you so much!
Little warriors are strong and brave,
One day you will have a kidney donor that's what I say.

Will I wait for years my doctor cannot say?
Then I heard the phone ring, one February day.
"Quick dial Alice's nurse" I heard my Dad shout.
My nurse screams, "we found a match I have no doubt"

21

I am blessed to receive a kidney.
A second chance at life
I am blessed to receive a kidney.
We put up a fight!

Special Thanks

Go Kidney Warriors!! Never ever give up!! Alice did not give up and her parents and her Dialysis Nurse did not give up on her either.

Special thanks to National Kidney Foundation, American Kidney Foundation, UNOS, and all other kidney organizations. Many thanks to all dialysis centers around the world, kidney doctors, transplant teams, and most importantly ***nurses.***